30 RE

for Beginners

A Super Simple Cookie Book

William David Welch

Think what a better world it would be if we all, the whole world, had cookies and milk about three o'clock every afternoon and then lay down on our blankets for a nap.

Barbara Jordan

Contents

ABOUT THIS
EASY COOKIE RECIPE BOOK

These 30 recipes are simple, quick and will leave your kitchen smelling great.

Perfect for friends and family for any occasion. From lunchbox snacks to teatime treats, each recipe is something special.

These recipes are so delicious that you shouldn't be surprised if you find yourself asking, "Who stole the cookie from the cookie jar?"

Ready, Set, Bake.

PEANUT BUTTER COOKIES

A classic cookie perfect for lunch boxes and picnics in the park

Easy-peasy

25 minutes

180kcal per cookie

36 cookies

INGREDIENTS

1 cup (250g) smooth peanut butter

1 cup (250g) shortening (room temperature)

1 cup (250g) white sugar

1 cup (250g) brown sugar

3 eggs (room temperature)

3 cups (250g) flour (all-purpose)

2 teaspoons (10g) baking soda

¼ teaspoon (2g) salt

BAKING STEPS

1. Preheat the oven to 375°F (190°C).

2. In a large mixing bowl, cream together the shortening, peanut butter and the sugars until they are light (5 mins).

3. Now add your eggs. Be sure to only add them one at a time and beat well after each egg is added.

4. Add your remaining dry ingredients (salt, flour, baking soda). Place them into the mixing bowl and add to creamed mixture and mix well.

5. Once your mixture is ready it is time to form your cookies. Roll the cookie dough into 1-1/2 inch (2-2.5cm) balls. On an ungreased tray, place the cookie dough balls about 3 inches (7.5cm) apart. Press each ball down with a fork.

6. Bake for about 10 to 15 minutes.

7. Once the cookies are golden brown remove them from the oven and place on wire racks until cool.

BAKING TOOLS

Baking Sheets, Cookie Canister, Measuring Spoons. Mixing Bowl, Measuring Cups, Stand Mixer, Fork, Wire Baking Racks

CHOCOLATE CHIP COOKIES

Another classic that everyone should have in their kitchen pantry

Easy-ish

45 minutes

311kcal per cookie

24 cookies

INGREDIENTS

1 cup (250g) softened butter

1 cup (250g) brown sugar

¾ cup (187g) sugar

2 eggs (room temperature)

1 teaspoon (5g) vanilla essence

2 2/3 cups (670g) all-purpose flour

1 1/4 teaspoons (7g) baking soda

1 teaspoon salt

12 ounces (340g) chocolate chips

2 cups (500g) walnuts (toasted and chopped)

BAKING STEPS

1. Combine softened butter and sugars in a mixing bowl until creamed. Then add the eggs and vanilla to the mixture. In another bowl, combine the flour, baking soda and salt. Slowly add this into the creamed mixture. Add in chopped walnuts and chocolate chips. Stir.

2. Shape roughly 1/4 cupfuls (62g each) of cookie dough into balls. (These are big cookies.)

3. Press each down into 3/4-inch (2cm) thickness. Place the cookie dough rounds into a plastic container. Use baking paper to separate the layers. Seal the container so it is airtight, and put it in the fridge overnight.

4. When you are ready to bake, line your baking trays with paper. Then place the cookie dough about 2 inches (5cm) apart. Allow the cookies to stand for 25-30 minutes before baking. Preheat the oven to 400°F (205°C).

5. Bake for 10-12 minutes. Once the cookies are golden brown at the edges, remove them from the oven and place them on wire racks until cool.

BAKING TOOLS

Baking Sheets, Cookie Canister, Measuring Spoons. Mixing Bowl, Measuring Cups, Stand Mixer, Baking Paper, Wire Baking Racks, Airtight Container

Coconut Macaroons

A must-bake for coconut-lovers

Easy-Peasy

30 minutes

54kcal per cookie

18 cookies

INGREDIENTS

1 1/3 cups (310g) shredded, sweetened coconut

1/3 cup (83g) white sugar

2 tablespoons (10g) all-purpose flour

1/8 teaspoon (0.6g) salt

2 egg whites at room temperature

1/2 teaspoon (2.5g) vanilla essence

BAKING STEPS

1. In a mixing bowl, add the shredded coconut, sugar, all-purpose flour, and salt.

2. In the same bowl, add the two egg whites and the vanilla essence; combine well.

3. Preheat your oven to 325°F (160°C).

4. Line your baking sheets with parchment paper. Drop teaspoons of macaroon dough onto the sheets about 2 inches (5cm) apart.

5. Bake for about 20 minutes or until the macaroons are a nice golden brown. Place on a wire rack until cookies are cooled.

6. Store in a cookie canister.

BAKING TOOLS

Baking Sheets, Cookie Canister, Measuring Spoons. Mixing Bowl, Measuring Cups, Stand Mixer, Baking Paper, Wire Baking Racks, Teaspoon

FESTIVE GINGER COOKIES

A wonderful Festive bake filled with warmth and comfort

Difficulty

30 minutes

111 kcal per cookie

30 cookies

INGREDIENTS

¾ cup (187g) softened butter

1 cup (25g) brown sugar

1 egg (room temperature)

¼ cup (62g) molasses

2 1/4 cups (560g) all-purpose flour

1 teaspoon (5g) baking soda

2 teaspoons (10g) ground ginger

1/2 teaspoon ground cloves

3/4 teaspoon (3g) ground cinnamon

¼ teaspoon (1.2g) salt

Extra sugar

BAKING STEPS

1. Cream the sugar and the butter together in a large mixing bowl.

2. In another large bowl, combine the egg and molasses. Add the flour, baking soda, cinnamon, ginger, cloves, and the salt to the butter-sugar mixture and combine.

3. Roll the cookie dough into 1 1/2-in. balls (2-2.5cm). Roll the balls in the extra sugar.

4. Place the balls roughly 2 inches (5cm) apart on baking trays. You don't need to grease the trays.

5. Bake at 350°F (180°C) for 10 minutes or until they are lightly browned.

6. Place on a baking rack until completely cool.

7. Store in a cookie canister.

BAKING TOOLS

Baking Sheets, Cookie Canister, Measuring Spoons. Mixing Bowl, Measuring Cups, Stand Mixer, Baking Paper, Wire Baking Racks, Rolling Pin

PECAN NUT COOKIES

A nutty, melt-in-the-mouth cookie that is a festive favorite

Easy-peasy

25 minutes

73 kcal per cookie

48 cookies

INGREDIENTS

1 cup (250g) softened butter

1/2 cup (250g) confectioners' sugar

1 teaspoon (5g) vanilla essence

2 1/4 cups (560g) all-purpose flour

1/4 teaspoon (2g) salt

3/4 cup (187g) pecans (chopped)

Extra confectioners' sugar

BAKING STEPS

1. Cream together the sugar and the softened butter until it is fluffy (about 5 minutes). Add in the vanilla essence.

2. In a different bowl, add the flour and salt. Then slowly add it to creamed butter and sugar. Add the pecans and stir. Put the dough in the refrigerator until chilled.

3. While the cookie dough is in the fridge, turn on your oven to 350°F (180°C) to preheat.

4. Roll your cookie dough into balls, roughly 1-inch (2.5cm) in size. Place them on baking trays. There is no need to grease the trays.

5. Bake for 10 minutes until set.

6. Roll the warm cookies in the extra confectioners' sugar and cool on wire racks. Afterwards, roll cooled cookies in extra sugar once again.

7. Store in a cookie canister.

BAKING TOOLS

Baking Sheets, Cookie Canister, Measuring Spoons. Mixing Bowl, Measuring Cups, Stand Mixer, Wire Baking Racks

AUTHENTIC SCOTTISH SHORTBREAD

A recipe all the way from the Scottish Highlands

Simple

35 minutes

40kcal per cookie

46 cookies

INGREDIENTS

2 cups (500g) softened butter

1 cup (250g) brown sugar

4 to 4 1/2 cups (1kg-1.25kg) all-purpose flour

BAKING STEPS

1. Preheat your oven to 325°F (160°C). Then combine the softened butter and the brown sugar and cream together until fluffy (5 mins). Add 3 3/4 cups of the all-purpose flour and mix well.

2. Place the shortbread dough onto a well-floured surface and knead for 4-5 minutes. While you knead, add the rest of the flour.

3. Roll the dough into 1/2-inch (2cm) thickness. Cut the dough into 3 x 1-inch (2.5cm) strips. Place them 1 inch (2.5cm) apart on ungreased baking sheets. Prick with a fork.

4. Bake the shortbread for around 20 minutes or until lightly golden. Cool on a wire rack.

5. Store in a cookie canister.

BAKING TOOLS

Baking Sheets, Cookie Canister, Measuring Spoons. Mixing Bowl, Measuring Cups, Stand Mixer, Wire Baking Racks, Fork, Knife

AMISH SUGAR COOKIES

A simple and delicious recipe for Amish-style cookies

Easy-Peasy

20 minutes

117kcal per cookie

60 cookies

INGREDIENTS

1 cup (250g) softened butter

1 cup (250g) vegetable oil

1 cup (250g) sugar

1 cup (250g) confectioners' sugar

2 eggs (room temperature)

1 teaspoon (5g) vanilla essence

4 1/2 cups(1.25kg) all-purpose flour

1 teaspoon (5g) baking soda

1 teaspoon (5g) cream of tartar

BAKING STEPS

1. Preheat oven your oven to 375°F (180°C).

2. In a large mixing bowl, combine the softened butter, vegetable oil and sugars. Then add the eggs and mix well. Add the vanilla essence before gradually combining the all-purpose flour, baking soda and cream of tartar.

3. Drop teaspoonfuls of dough onto the ungreased baking sheets.

4. Bake for 8-10 minutes or until the cookies are lightly browned.

5. Remove and place on baking racks to cool.

6. Store in a cookie canister.

BAKING TOOLS

Baking Sheets, Cookie Canister, Measuring Spoons. Mixing Bowl, Measuring Cups, Stand Mixer, Wire Baking Racks, Teaspoon

OATMEAL COOKIES

A classic oatmeal cookie recipe with a chocolate twist

Easy-ish

30 minutes

87kcal per cookie

84 cookies

INGREDIENTS

1 cup (250g) softened butter

3/4 cup (182g) sugar

3/4 cup (182g) packed brown sugar

2 extra-large eggs

1 teaspoon (5g) vanilla essence

3 cups (750g) quick-cook oats

1 1/2 cups (750g) all-purpose flour

3.4 ounces instant vanilla pudding mix

1 teaspoon (5g) baking soda

1 teaspoon (5g) salt

2 cups (500g) chocolate chips

1 cup (500g) chopped nuts

BAKING STEPS

1. Cream together the two sugars and the softened butter in a mixing bowl. Then add eggs and vanilla and beat.

2. In another bowl, add the oats, all-purpose flour, pudding mix, baking soda, and salt. Combine and slowly add to creamed mixture while mixing. Add in chocolate chips and the chopped nuts.

3. Use a leveled tablespoon to drop the oatmeal cookie dough onto an ungreased baking sheet. Place the dough 2 inches (5cm) apart.

4. Bake at 375°F (190°C) for 10 minutes or until the cookies are lightly browned.

5. Remove and allow to cool on baking racks.

6. Store in a cookie canister.

BAKING TOOLS

Baking Sheets, Cookie Canister, Measuring Spoons. Mixing Bowl, Measuring Cups, Stand Mixer, Wire Baking Racks, Teaspoon

SNICKERDOODLES

A cookie that is as fun to say as it is to eat

Easy Peasy

30 minutes

81 kcal per cookie

30 cookies

INGREDIENTS

1/2 cup (125g) softened butter

1 cup (250g) + 2 tablespoons (40g) sugar

1 egg (room temperature)

1/2 teaspoon (2.5g) vanilla essence

1 1/2 cups (750g) all-purpose flour

1/4 teaspoon (1.5g) baking soda

1/4 teaspoon (1.5g) cream of tartar

1 teaspoon (5g) ground cinnamon

BAKING STEPS

1. Preheat your oven to 375°F (190°C).

2. Cream together the butter and 1 cup of the sugar until fluffy. Then add the egg and vanilla essence.

3. In a separate bowl, add together flour, baking soda and cream of tartar. Then slowly add to the creamed mixture.

4. In a smaller bowl, combine the ground cinnamon and the rest of the sugar.

5. Shape the cookie dough into 1-inch (2.5cm) balls. Gently roll the balls in the cinnamon/sugar mixture. Place the balls on ungreased baking sheets about 2 inches (5cm) apart.

6. Bake for 10-12 minutes until lightly browned.

7. Remove and cool on baking racks.

8. Store in a cookie canister.

BAKING TOOLS

Baking Sheets, Cookie Canister, Measuring Spoons. Mixing Bowl, Measuring Cups, Stand Mixer, Wire Baking Racks, Tablespoon, Whisk

LEMON COOKIES

A fluffy cookie with a delicious lemon filling

Easy-ish

35 minutes

70 kcal per cookie

45 cookies

INGREDIENTS

1/4 cup (62g) softened butter

1/2 cup (125g) sugar

1 egg yolk at room temperature

1/2 teaspoon (2.5g) vanilla essence

2 cups (500g) all-purpose flour

1/4 cup (62g) walnuts (finely chopped)

FILLING:

3 tablespoons (60g) softened butter

4 teaspoon (20g) lemon juice

1 teaspoon (5g) grated orange zest.

1 1/2 cups (375g) confectioners' sugar

BAKING STEPS

1. Cream the sugar and softened butter in a mixing bowl until light and fluffy (5 mins). After that, whisk together the egg yolk and vanilla extract. Slowly drizzle in the flour and stir to mix.

2. Cut the dough into two pieces and roll each piece into a 14-inch (35-centimeter) roll. Cover in clingfilm and refrigerate overnight.

3. Remove the wrapper and cut it into 1/4-inch strips. Place roughly 2 inches (5cm) apart on ungreased trays. Half of the cookie should be sprinkled.

4. Bake for 8-10 minutes at 400°F (204°C) or until golden brown around the edges. Ensure they are completely cooled on wire racks.

5. Cream the sugar, lemon juice, and orange zest together in a small bowl until fluffy. Gradually stir in the confectioners' sugar until it is fully smooth. If desired, tint yellow. Spread around 1 teaspoon filling on plain cookies' bottoms, then top with nut-topped cookies.

BAKING TOOLS

Baking Sheets, Cookie Canister, Measuring Spoons. Mixing Bowl, Measuring Cups, Stand Mixer, Wire Baking Racks, Tablespoon, Whisk

DELICATE MERINGUE COOKIES

Pretty and decadent little cookies that are as light as air

Easy-ish

60 minutes

Category

60 cookies

INGREDIENTS

3 extra-large egg whites

1 1/2 (7g) teaspoons clear or regular vanilla essence

1/4 (2g) teaspoon cream of tartar

A pinch of salt

2/3 cup (167g) sugar

BAKING STEPS

1. Put the egg whites into a bowl and set aside for 30 minutes at room temperature.

2. Preheat the oven to 250°F (120°C). Toss the egg whites with the vanilla, cream of tartar, and salt and beat on medium speed until foamy. One tablespoon at a time, add sugar, beating on high after each addition until sugar is dissolved. Continue beating for another 7 minutes, or until stiff glossy peaks form.

3. Place a #32-star piping tip into a pierced, food-safe plastic bag. Pour the meringue in the bag. Pipe 1 1/4-inch diameter cookies, 2 inches apart, onto parchment-lined baking sheets.

4. Bake for around 40 minutes. They should be firm to the touch. Switch off the oven and leave the meringues in for 1 hour (leave the oven door closed). Remove from oven and place on trays. Remove the meringues from the paper and store them in an airtight jar at room temperature.

BAKING TOOLS

Baking Sheets, Cookie Canister, Measuring Spoons. Mixing Bowl, Measuring Cups, Stand Mixer, Wire Baking Racks, Tablespoon, Icing bag, #32-star tip

STICKY MOLASSES COOKIES

A warm, sweet, smoky cookie with a spicy crunch

Easy-peasy

45 minutes

310kcal per cookie

24 cookies

INGREDIENTS

1 1/2 cups (375g) softened butter

2 cups (500g) sugar

2 eggs at room temperature

1/2 cup (125g) molasses

4 1/2 (1.25kg) cups all-purpose flour

4 teaspoons (20g) ginger

2 teaspoons (10g) baking soda

1 1/2 teaspoon (8g) ground cinnamon

1 teaspoon (5g) ground cloves

Pinch of salt

1/4 cup (63g) chopped pecans

3/4 cup (187g) coarse sugar

BAKING STEPS

1. Preheat the oven to 350°F (180°C).

2. Cream the sugar and softened butter together in a mixing bowl until fluffy.

3. Whisk together the eggs and molasses in a separate bowl. Combine the flour, ginger, baking soda, cinnamon, cloves, and salt in a mixing bowl; gradually apply to the creamed mixture and combine thoroughly. Pecans should be folded in at this stage.

4. Roll in coarse sugar and shape into 2-inch balls. Place on ungreased baking sheets 2 1/2 in. apart. Bake for 13-15 minutes, or until the tops of the cookies are cracked. Remove to wire racks until completely cooled.

BAKING TIPS

Baking Sheets, Cookie Canister, Measuring Spoons. Mixing Bowl, Measuring Cups, Stand Mixer, Wire Baking Racks, Tablespoon, Paddle for folding

BANANA CHOCOLATE CHIP COOKIES

Bananas and chocolate were always meant to be combined into a cookie

Easy-peasy

35 minutes

Category

36 cookies

INGREDIENTS

1/3 cup (83g) softened butter

½ cup (125g) sugar

1 egg at room temperature

1/2 cup (125g) mashed banana

1/2 teaspoon (2.5g) vanilla essence

1 1/4 cups (312g) all-purpose flour

1 teaspoon (5g) baking soda

Pinch of salt

1 cup (250g) semisweet chocolate chips

BAKING STEPS

1. Cream the sugar and softened butter in a mixing bowl until fluffy. Whisk together the egg, banana, and vanilla extract in another bowl.

2. Combine the rest of the dry ingredients including the flour, baking powder, and salt; gradually apply to the creamed mixture, mixing well with each addition. Add the chocolate chips and blend.

3. Prepare baking trays by spraying with baking spray. Drop dough by the tablespoon onto baking trays. Space them 2 inches (5cm) apart.

4. Bake for 15 minutes until they are lightly browned on the edges, at 350°F (180°C). Place on wire racks until completely cooled.

BAKING TOOLS

Baking Sheets, Cookie Canister, Measuring Spoons. Mixing Bowl, Measuring Cups, Stand Mixer, Wire Baking Racks, Tablespoon, Whisk, Cooking Spray

Butter Cookies

A classic Danish recipe made right at home

| Easy-Peasy | 35 minutes | 173 kcal per cookie | 72 cookies |

INGREDIENTS

1 cup (25g) softened butter (lightly salted)

¾ (187g) cup sugar

1 egg at room temperature

1/2 teaspoon (2.5g) vanilla essence

2 1/2 cups (625g) all-purpose flour

1 teaspoon (5g) baking powder

Pinch of salt

BAKING STEPS

1. Turn on your oven to 375°F (190°C) to preheat.

2. In a bowl, cream sugar and butter together for 5 minutes. Add in the egg and vanilla essence.

3. Whisk flour, baking powder and salt together. Slowly beat into the creamed mixture.

4. Press the cookie doughs 1 inch (2cm) apart onto ungreased baking using a heart-shaped disk fitting.

5. Bake for 7-8 minutes until set.

6. Place on baking racks.

7. For the icing, beat together the butter, confectioners' sugar, vanilla and milk. You want to have a spreading consistency. You may tint the icing with food coloring.

8. Decorate the cookies as desired.

BAKING TOOLS

Baking Sheets, Cookie Canister, Measuring Spoons. Mixing Bowl, Measuring Cups, Stand Mixer, Wire Baking Racks, Tablespoon, Cooking spray

ICED GINGERSNAPS

Everyone loves a cookie with a good "snap"

Easy-ish

30 minutes

47kcal per cookie

160 Servings

INGREDIENTS

2 cups (500g) sugar

1 1/2 cups (375g) canola oil

2 eggs at room temperature

1/2 cup (125g) molasses

4 cups (1kg) all-purpose flour

4 teaspoons (25g) baking soda

3 teaspoons (15g) ground ginger

2 teaspoons (10g) ground cinnamon

Extra sugar

24 ounces (680g) white chocolate baking chips

1/4 cup (62g) shortening
Pinch of salt

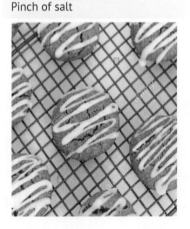

BAKING STEPS

1. Add sugar and oil in a large mixing bowl. Incorporate the eggs. Add the molasses and blend well.

2. Combine the flour, baking soda, ginger, cinnamon, and salt in a mixing bowl; gradually apply to the creamed mixture and combine thoroughly.

3. Shape into 3/4 inch balls and roll in extra sugar. Place them roughly 2 inches (5cm) apart on baking trays that have not been greased. Bake at 350°F (180°C) for 10 minutes. Set out to cool on wire racks.

4. Melt both chocolate chips and the shortening in the microwave and stir until smooth. Enable excess to drip off after dipping cookies halfway into the melted chips or drizzling with the mixture. Place on waxed paper and set aside to dry.

BAKING TOOLS

Baking Sheets, Cookie Canister, Measuring Spoons. Mixing Bowl, Measuring Cups, Stand Mixer, Wire Baking Racks, Tablespoon, Wax Paper

CHOCOLATE AND NUT BISCOTTI

You now do not need to travel to Italy for delicious biscotti

| Easy-ish | 70 minutes | 134kcal per cookie | 30 cookies |

INGREDIENTS

3/4 cup (187g) sugar

1/2 cup (125g) canola oil

2 extra-large eggs (room temp)

1 teaspoon (5g) vanilla essence

1 3/4 cups (440g) all-purpose flour

1 1/2 teaspoons (8g) baking powder

1/2 teaspoon salt

3/4 cup (187g) white baking chips

3/4 cup (187g) dried cranberries

3/4 cup (187g) pistachios

BAKING STEPS

1. Preheat oven to 325°F (160°C). Sugar and oil should be mixed in a small tub. In a separate cup, whisk together the eggs and vanilla extract. Combine the flour, baking powder, and salt in a mixing bowl; gradually incorporate the sugar mixture and thoroughly combine. Combine with the chips, cranberries, and pistachios into a mixing bowl.

2. Split the dough into two pieces. Shape each portion of dough into a 10 x 1 1/2 inch rectangle on a parchment-lined baking sheet with lightly floured hands. Bake for 30–35 minutes in the oven.

3. Place the pans on wire racks to cool. Move rectangles to a cutting board when cool enough to handle; cut diagonally into 1/2-inch slices with a serrated knife.

4. Place the slices on baking sheets, cut side down. Bake for 6-7 minutes per hand, or until golden brown on both sides. Cool completely on wire racks. Keep the jar airtight.

BAKING TOOLS

Baking Sheets, Cookie Canister, Measuring Spoons. Mixing Bowl, Measuring Cups, Stand Mixer, Wire Baking Racks, Tablespoon, Baking Pans, Serrated Knife

RED VELVET COOKIES

We fell in love with the cake, now it's time for the cookie

Easy-ish

30 minutes

103kcal per cookie

60 cookies

INGREDIENTS

2 ounces (57g) unsweetened chocolate

1/2 cup (125g) softened butter

2/3 cup (187g) brown sugar

1/3 cup (83g) white sugar

1 extra large egg (room temperature)

1 tablespoon (10g) red food coloring

1 teaspoon (5g) vanilla essence

2 cups (500g) all-purpose flour

1/2 teaspoon (2.5g) baking soda

1/2 teaspoon (2.5g) salt

1 cup (250g) sour cream

1 cup (250g) semisweet chocolate chips

BAKING STEPS

1. In a microwave, melt the unsweetened chocolate and then stir until smooth.

2. Cream butter and sugars in a wide mixing bowl until light and fluffy, around 5-7 minutes. In another bowl, whisk together the egg, food coloring, and vanilla extract.

3. Add in the cooled chocolate and beat until smooth. Add the flour, baking soda, and the salt in a different bowl; alternate adding in the flour mixture and sour cream to the creamed mixture, beating well with each addition. Fold in the chocolate chips and blend well.

4. Drop by tablespoonfuls onto parchment-lined baking sheets, 2 inches (5cm) apart. Preheat your oven to 375°F (190°C) and bake for 6-9 minutes, or until set. Set and cool completely on wire racks. Using frosting, cover the cake. Sprinkles may be topped, if desired.

BAKING TOOLS

Baking Sheets, Cookie Canister, Measuring Spoons. Mixing Bowl, Measuring Cups, Stand Mixer, Wire Baking Racks, Tablespoon

CITRUS SNOWFLAKES

A zesty, delicate cookie perfect for teatime

| Easy-peasy | 40 minutes | 37 kcal per cookie | 65 cookies |

INGREDIENTS

1 packet of lemon cake mix (430g)

2 1/4 cups (562g) whipped topping.

1 extra-large egg at room temperature

Confectioners' sugar for dusting

BAKING STEPS

1. Combine the cake mix, whipped topping, and egg in a large mixing bowl and mix well. The batter should be very sticky.

2. Drop teaspoonfuls into a bowl of confectioners' sugar and roll gently to coat. Place on baking sheets that have not been greased.

3. Bake for 10-12 minutes at 350°F (180°C) or until tops are lightly browned and cracked. Set out to cool on wire racks.

BAKING TOOLS

Baking Sheets, Cookie Canister, Measuring Spoons. Mixing Bowl, Measuring Cups, Stand Mixer, Wire Baking Racks, Tablespoon

HOBNOB COOKIES

A British classic. So, let's "hobnob" over coffee and biscuits.

| Easy | 40 minutes | 67kcal per cookie | 30 cookies |

INGREDIENTS

1½ cups (375g) all-purpose flour

1½ cups (375g) old-fashioned oats

1½ teaspoons (8g) baking soda.

1½ teaspoons (8g) salt

1 cup (250g) unsalted, softened butter

1 cup (250g) sugar

2 tablespoons (40g) whole milk

2 teaspoons (10g) honey

COOKING STEPS

1. Start by preheating your oven to 300°F (150°C).

2. In a medium mixing bowl, add flour, oats, baking soda, and salt. Mix for 3 minutes on medium-high speed with an electric mixer; beat butter and sugar until light and fluffy. In a mixing dish, combine the milk and honey. Switch off the mixer and whisk in all the ingredients with a rubber spatula.

3. Place heaping tablespoonfuls of dough on two parchment-lined baking sheets and gently press down and space them 1½ inch (2.5cm) apart.

4. Bake for around 25minutes, until they are golden brown (they will crisp as they cool). Place the baking sheets on a wire rack to cool.

5. Cookies can be baked up to a week ahead of time. Store in an airtight jar at room temperature.

BAKING TOOLS

Baking Sheets, Cookie Canister, Measuring Spoons. Mixing Bowl, Measuring Cups, Stand Mixer, Wire Baking Racks, Rubber Spatula, Parchment Paper

PEANUT BUTTER SANDWICH COOKIE

A fresh take on a peanut butter sandwich, which will be a huge lunchbox hit

Easy-ish

30 minutes

197cal per cookie

44 Servings

INGREDIENTS

1 cup (250g) butter-flavored shortening

1 cup (250g) creamy peanut butter

1 cup (250g) sugar

1 cup (250g) brown sugar

3 extra-large eggs

1 teaspoon (5g) vanilla essence

3 cups (750g) all-purpose flour

2 teaspoons (10g) baking soda

1/4 teaspoon (1.2g) salt

FILLING:

1/2 cup (125g) creamy peanut butter

3 cups (750g) confectioners' sugar

1 teaspoon (5g) vanilla essence

5 to 6 tablespoons (100g) milk

BAKING STEPS

1. Cream together your peanut butter, sugars and shortening in a mixing bowl until light and fluffy, around 4 minutes. In another dish, whisk up the eggs and vanilla essence. Combine the flour, baking soda, and salt, blend into the creamed mixture until thoroughly mixed.

2. Roll into 1-inch balls and place 2 inches apart on baking sheets that have not been greased. With a fork, flatten to 3/8-inch thickness. Bake at 375° (190°C) for 7-8 minutes, or until golden. Transfer to a wire rack to cool.

3. To make the filling, add the peanut butter, confectioners' sugar, vanilla, and enough milk to achieve a spreading consistency in a large mixing bowl. One cookie should be spread with the filling, and then topped with another cookie.

BAKING TOOLS

Baking Sheets, Cookie Canister, Measuring Spoons. Mixing Bowl, Measuring Cups, Stand Mixer, Wire Baking Racks, Rubber Spatula, Parchment Paper

TOFFEE ALMOND COOKIES

A chewy, nutty, decadent cookie

Easy-peasy

50 minutes

68kcal per cookie

140 cookies

INGREDIENTS

1 cup (250g) softened butter

1 cup (250g) sugar

1 cup (250g) confectioners' sugar

1 cup (250g) canola oil

2 extra-large eggs

1 teaspoon (5g) almond essence

3 1/2 (875g) cups all-purpose flour

1 cup (250g) whole wheat flour

1 teaspoon (5g) baking soda

1 teaspoon (5g) cream of tartar

2 cups (500g) chopped almonds.

8 ounces (230g) milk chocolate English toffee bits

Extra sugar

BAKING STEPS

1. Start by creaming the butter and sugars in a mixing bowl until light and fluffy. Combine the oil, eggs, and essence. Add the flours, the baking soda, cream of tartar, and the salt into a mixing bowl; gradually add to the creamed mixture and thoroughly combine. Add the almonds and toffee bits and blend well.

2. Roll in extra sugar and shape into 1-inch balls. Place on baking sheets that have not been greased and flatten with a fork. Turn on your oven to 350°F (180°C) to preheat. Bake for 12-14 minutes, or until lightly browned.

BAKING TOOLS

Baking Sheets, Cookie Canister, Measuring Spoons. Mixing Bowl, Measuring Cups, Stand Mixer, Wire Baking Racks, Fork

THUMBPRINT COOKIES

Make these your signature cookies; you won't be sorry

Easy

35 minutes

73 kcal per cookie

30 cookies

INGREDIENTS

6 tablespoons (120g) softened butter

1/2 cup (125g) sugar

1 extra-large egg (room temp)

2 tablespoons (40g) canola oil

1 teaspoon (5g) vanilla extract

1/4 teaspoon (1.2g) butter flavoring

1 1/2 cups (375g) all-purpose flour

1/4 cup (62g) cornstarch

1 teaspoon (5g) baking powder

¼ teaspoon(2g) salt

3 tablespoons (60g) raspberry/strawberry or other fruit preserves

BAKING STEPS

1. Begin by preheating the oven to 350°F (180°C).

2. Cream the sugar and butter together until light and fluffy; add the egg, oil, vanilla, and butter flavoring and blend well. Combine the all-purpose flour, the cornstarch, the baking powder, and the salt in a separate bowl; gradually beat into creamed mixture.

3. Roll dough into 1-inch balls and put-on greased baking sheets 2 inches apart. With the end of a wooden spoon handle, make a deep indentation in the middle of each. Spoon preserves onto each cookie.

4. Bake until for 10-12 minutes or until the cookie is a golden-brown color.

5. Remove them from the oven and place on wire racks until cool.

BAKING TOOLS

Baking Sheets, Cookie Canister, Measuring Spoons. Mixing Bowl, Measuring Cups, Stand Mixer, Wire Baking Racks, Wooden Spoon

MACADAMIA COOKIES

This recipe is "nutting" but goodness

Easy

25 minutes

70kcal per cookie

54 cookies

INGREDIENTS

1/2 cup (125g) softened butter

2/3 cup (187g) sugar

1 extra-large egg

1 teaspoon (5g) vanilla essence

1 cup (250g) all-purpose flour

1/2 teaspoon (2.5g) baking soda

1 cup (250g) chopped macadamia nuts

1 cup (250g) white baking chips

BAKING STEPS

1. Preheat the oven to 350°F (180°C). Begin by creaming the softened butter and sugar together in a mixing bowl until light and fluffy. In a separate bowl, whisk up the egg and vanilla extract. In a separate cup, whisk together the flour and baking soda; progressively incorporate into the creamed mixture. Add in the nuts and baking chips and combine well.

2. Drop heaping teaspoonfuls onto ungreased baking sheets 2 inches apart. Preheat oven to 350°F and bake for 10-12 minutes, or until golden brown. Cool for 1 minute on the pans. Transfer to wire racks to cool.

BAKING TOOLS

Baking Sheets, Cookie Canister, Measuring Spoons. Mixing Bowl, Measuring Cups, Stand Mixer, Wire Baking Racks, Wooden Spoon

GLUTEN-FREE CHOCOLATE CHIP COOKIE

A classic that now everyone can enjoy

easy

25 minutes

117kcal per cookie

22 cookies

INGREDIENTS

1 1/4 cups (312g) Gluten-free Baking Flour

1/2 teaspoon (2.5g) baking soda

1/4 teaspoon (1.2g) salt

6 tablespoons butter (120g)

1/2 cup (125g) dark brown sugar

1/4 cup (62g) sugar

1 teaspoon (5g) vanilla essence

1 extra-large egg

1 cup (250g) chocolate chips

BAKING STEPS

1. Turn on the oven to 350°F (180°C) to preheat. Line two baking trays with parchment paper.

2. In a bowl, combine the flour, baking soda, and salt. Add the melted butter, dark brown sugar, sugar, and vanilla extract in a large mixing bowl. Blend until smooth.

3. Add each of the eggs one by one, making sure to mix well after each addition. The final product should imitate a thick caramel sauce. Enable the mixer to come to a halt before adding the flour. Mix again until a dense dough forms on medium speed. Mix in the chocolate chips.

4. Drop two tablespoons of dough onto each prepared cookie sheet. Bake until golden.

BAKING TOOLS

Baking Sheets, Cookie Canister, Measuring Spoons. Mixing Bowl, Measuring Cups, Stand Mixer, Wire Baking Racks, Tablespoons

CRANBERRY OATMEAL COOKIES

A classic oatmeal cookie with a healthy and delicious twist

| Easy-peasy | 26 minutes | 89kcal per cookie | 72 cookies |

INGREDIENTS

1 cup (250g) softened butter

1 1/2 cups (375g) sugar

2 extra-large eggs

1 teaspoon (5g) vanilla essence

2 cups (500g) all-purpose flour

1 teaspoon (5g) baking powder

1/2 teaspoon (2.5g) salt

1/4 teaspoon (1.2g) baking soda

2 cups (500g) quick-cook oats

1 cup (250g) raisins

1 cup (500g) fresh or frozen cranberries - chopped

1 tablespoon grated orange zest

12 ounces (340g) white baking chips

BAKING STEPS

1. Start by creaming together the softened butter and sugar in a mixing bowl until light and fluffy.

2. One at a time, add the eggs, beating well after each addition. Blend in the vanilla essence. Add the flour, the baking powder, the salt, as well as the baking soda to the creamed mixture and whisk to blend. Combine the oats, raisins, cranberries, and orange zest in a mixing dish. Add the baking chips and blend well.

3. Drop rounded teaspoonfuls of cookie dough onto greased baking sheets, spacing them about 2 inches (5cm) apart.

BAKING TOOLS

Baking Sheets, Cookie Canister, Measuring Spoons. Mixing Bowl, Measuring Cups, Stand Mixer, Wire Baking Racks, Tablespoons

GLUTEN-FREE SUGAR COOKIES

So delicious that no one will guess they are gluten-free

| Easy | 87 minutes | 136 kcal per cookie | 24 cookies |

INGREDIENTS

1 cup (250g) sugar

½ cup (125g) softened butter

1 extra-large egg

1 tablespoon (10g) water

1 ½ teaspoons (8g) vanilla essence

Pinch of salt

½ teaspoon (2g) xanthan gum (leave out if in flour)

2 cups (500g) gluten-free all-purpose flour

Extra flour for rolling and dusting

BAKING STEPS

1. Combine sugar and butter in a mixing bowl on medium speed. Make sure they are creamed. Then combine the egg, vanilla, salt, and cinnamon (if using) in a mixing bowl. Mix until well blended.

2. Add the flour and xanthan gum (if using). Mix on low speed until well blended. Cover and refrigerate for at least 1 hour.

3. Preheat the oven to 350°F (180°C). Roll out the dough to a thickness of approximately 14 inches (36cm) in length on a lightly floured surface.

4. Print out the cookies with cookie cutters of your choosing and put them on the baking sheet. Make sure the cookies do not touch.

5. After reforming and rolling out the scrap dough, continue cutting more cookies. Bake for 10 to 12 minutes. Cool completely before attempting to decorate.

6. Keep for up to 5 days in an airtight jar.

BAKING TOOLS

Baking Sheets, Cookie Canister, Measuring Spoons. Mixing Bowl, Measuring Cups, Stand Mixer, Wire Baking Racks, Tablespoon, Cutting Board

RASPBERRY FINGERS

A buttery, melt-in-the-mouth cookie with a raspberry center

| Easy-peasy | 40 minutes | 67kcal per cookie | 60 Servings |

INGREDIENTS

1 cup (250g) softened butter

1/2 cup (125g) sugar

1 extra-large egg

1 teaspoon (5g) vanilla essence

2 1/4 cups (560g) all-purpose flour

1/2 teaspoon (2.5g) baking powder

Pinch of salt

1/2 cup (250g) raspberry jam

GLAZE:

1 cup (250g) confectioners' sugar

2 tablespoons (20g) evaporated milk

1/2 teaspoon (2.5g) vanilla essence

BAKING STEPS

1. Preheat your oven to 350°F (180°C).

2. Cream butter and granulated sugar in a large mixing bowl until light and fluffy, around 5-7 minutes. Whisk the egg and vanilla essence together. Combine flour, baking powder, and salt in a bowl; gradually apply to the creamed mixture and combine well.

3. Divide the dough into four portions and roll each into a 10-by-2 1/4 inch (5cm) log. Place on greased or foil-lined baking sheets 4 inches (10cm) apart with a depression down the center of each log. Bake for 10 minutes in the oven.

4. Place jam in the depressions. Bake for approx. 10 more minutes. Enable 2 minutes to cool. Place on a cutting board and slice into 3/4-inch slices. Place on a wire rack to cool.

5. Combine the glaze ingredients in a small tub. Drizzle the glaze over the warm cookies. Allow to cool completely.

BAKING TOOLS

Baking Sheets, Cookie Canister, Measuring Spoons. Mixing Bowl, Measuring Cups, Stand Mixer, Wire Baking Racks, Tablespoon, Cutting Board

BIG BROWNIE COOKIES

"Big" and "Brownie" should always precede "Cookie"

| Easy | 35 minutes | 350kcal per cookie | 18 cookies |

INGREDIENTS

2 2/3 cups (667g) of bittersweet chocolate chips
1/2 cup (125g) of unsalted butter
4 extra-large eggs (room temp)
1 1/2 cups (375g) of sugar
4 teaspoons (20g) vanilla essence
2/3 cup (187g) of all-purpose flour
1/2 teaspoon (2.5g) of baking powder
Pinch of salt
12 ounces (340g) of semisweet chocolate chunks.
1/2 teaspoon (2.5g) espresso powder (if desired)

BAKING STEPS

1. Preheat the oven to 350°F(180°C). Melt butter and chocolate chips in a saucepan over low heat, stirring continuously until smooth. Remove and set aside to cool until the mixture is warm.

2. In a small mixing cup, whisk together the eggs, sugar, vanilla, and espresso powder, if using. Incorporate the chocolate mixture with a brush. Combine the all-purpose flour, the baking powder, and the salt in a separate bowl, blend into the chocolate mixture until thoroughly mixed.

3. Stir in the chocolate chunks and set aside for 10 minutes, or until the mixture has thickened slightly.

4. Drop by 1/4 cupfuls onto parchment-lined baking sheets, 3 in. apart. Bake for 12-14 minutes, or until set. Cool for 1-2 minutes on the pans. Enable to cool further on wire racks.

BAKING TOOLS

Baking Sheets, Cookie Canister, Measuring Spoons. Mixing Bowl, Measuring Cups, Stand Mixer, Wire Baking Racks, Tablespoons, Parchment Paper, Pastry Brush

MINTY MELTS

Mint may not be for everyone, but these minty melts will certainly change your mind

| Easy-ish | 30 minutes | 126kcal per cookie | 40 Servings |

INGREDIENTS

1 cup (250g) softened butter

½ cup (125g) confectioners' sugar

1/2 teaspoon (2.5g) peppermint extract

1 1/4 cups (312g) all-purpose flour

1/2 cup (125g) cornstarch

FROSTING:

2 tablespoons (40g) softened butter

2 tablespoons (40g) milk

1/4 teaspoon (1.2g) peppermint essence

1 1/2 cups (375g) confectioners' sugar

1/2 cup (125g) crushed peppermint candies

BAKING STEPS

1. Cream butter and confectioners' sugar together in a small mixing bowl until light and fluffy. Mix in the extract. In a separate cup, whisk together the flour and cornstarch; gradually apply to the creamed mixture. Refrigerate for 30 minutes, sealed, or until the mixture is solid enough to treat.

2. Turn the oven on to 350°F (180°C) to preheat. Shape dough into 1-inch balls (2cm) and place them on ungreased baking sheets 2 inches (5cm) apart. Bake for around 10 minutes. Allow to cool on wire racks.

3. For the frosting, cream the softened butter until smooth. Mix in the milk, extract, and food coloring, if desired. Gradually add confectioners' sugar until fully smooth. Sprinkle smashed candies over the top of the cookies. Keep the jar airtight or cookie canister.

BAKING TOOLS

Baking Sheets, Cookie Canister, Measuring Spoons. Mixing Bowl, Measuring Cups, Stand Mixer, Wire Baking Racks, Tablespoon

GLUTEN-FREE KISS COOKIES

Free from Gluten but not free from taste

Easy-ish

30 minutes

98kcal per cookie

48 Servings

INGREDIENTS

1/4 cup (62g) butter-flavored shortening

1 1/4 cups (312g) brown sugar

3/4 cup (187g) peanut butter

1 extra-large egg (room temp)

1/4 cup (62g) of unsweetened applesauce

3 teaspoons (15g) vanilla extract

1 cup (250g) of white rice flour

1/2 cup (125g) of potato starch

1/4 cup (62g) of tapioca flour

1 teaspoon (10g) baking powder

3/4 teaspoon (4g) of baking soda

48 milk chocolate kisses
Pinch of salt

BAKING STEPS

1. In a large-sized mixing bowl, begin by creaming together the shortening, brown sugar, and peanut butter until smooth.

2. Combine the egg, applesauce, and vanilla extract in a mixing bowl (mixture will appear curdled). Rice flour, potato starch, tapioca flour, baking powder, baking soda, and salt are whisked together in a separate bowl and gradually added into the creamed mixture. Refrigerate for 1 hour, sealed tight.

3. Turn the oven to 375°F (190°C). Shape dough into 48 1-inch balls and space them 2 inches apart on ungreased baking sheets.

4. Bake for around 10 minutes, or until the surface is slightly broken. Place a chocolate kiss in the center of each cookie right away. Enable 2 minutes to cool on the pans. Allow to cool completely on wire racks.

BAKING TOOLS

Baking Sheets, Cookie Canister, Measuring Spoons. Mixing Bowl, Measuring Cups, Stand Mixer, Wire Baking Racks, Tablespoon

Happy baking!

Printed in Great Britain
by Amazon